THE TRUTH ABOUT Relationships

Loveland, Colorado

The Truth About Relationships
Core Belief Bible Study Series
Copyright © 1998 Group Publishing, Inc.

All rights reserved. No part of this book may be reproduced in any manner whatsoever without prior written permission from the publisher, except where noted in the text and in the case of brief quotations embodied in critical articles and reviews. For information, write Permissions, Group Publishing, Inc., Dept. PD, P.O. Box 481, Loveland, CO 80539.

Credits
Editors: Karl Leuthauser and Michael D. Warden
Creative Development Editors: Ivy Beckwith and Paul Woods
Chief Creative Officer: Joani Schultz
Copy Editor: Betty Taylor
Art Director: Ray Tollison
Cover Art Director: Jeff A. Storm
Computer Graphic Artist/Illustrator: Eris Klein
Photographer: Jafe Parsons
Production Manager: Gingar Kunkel

Unless otherwise noted, Scripture taken from the HOLY BIBLE, NEW INTERNATIONAL VERSION®. Copyright © 1973, 1978, 1984 by International Bible Society. Used by permission of Zondervan Publishing House. All rights reserved.

ISBN 0-7644-0872-0

10 9 8 7 6 5 4 3 2   07 06 05 04 03 02 01 00

Printed in the United States of America.

Visit our Web site: www.grouppublishing.com

contents:

the Core Belief: Relationships

God created us to live in relationship with one another, and because we're each unique, he created a variety of relationships we can enjoy—family, friends, co-workers, and neighbors. Being in relationship with others carries obligations, and we should all grant one another basic considerations such as love, respect, honesty, and forgiveness. As Christians, we should love, serve, and support one another and strive to maintain positive relationships with non-Christians to draw them into relationship with Jesus Christ.

the Helpful Stuff

RELATIONSHIPS AS A CORE CHRISTIAN BELIEF **7**
(or We're All in This Together)

ABOUT CORE BELIEF BIBLE STUDY SERIES **10**
(or How to Move Mountains in One Hour or Less)

WHY ACTIVE AND INTERACTIVE LEARNING WORKS WITH TEENAGERS **55**
(or How to Keep Your Kids Awake)

YOUR EVALUATION **61**
(or How You Can Edit Our Stuff Without Getting Paid)

the ▼Studies

Lean on Me — 15
THE ISSUE: Friendship
THE BIBLE CONNECTION: 1 Samuel 18:1-4; 20:1-42
THE POINT: Friends commit to helping each other.

"I Would Die for You" — 25
THE ISSUE: Gangs
THE BIBLE CONNECTION: Genesis 37:18-35; 1 Samuel 22:1-2; 24:3-7; Nehemiah 4:7-23; and John 15:12-17
THE POINT: True friends inspire excellence.

Winner Take All — 35
THE ISSUE: Competition
THE BIBLE CONNECTION: Genesis 13:5-9; Exodus 3:11-14; 4:10-16; 6:28–7:6; 12:50-51; 1 Samuel 1:3-11, 21-28; 2:19-21; 18:5-9, 12-13; 19:1-10; 20:1-4, 12-17; and John 3:22-30
THE POINT: Comparing yourself to others is destructive.

Friendship First — 45
THE ISSUE: Dating
THE BIBLE CONNECTION: 1 Samuel 16:7; John 13:34-35; Romans 12:10, 16; 14:19; Philippians 1:9-10; 1 Timothy 5:2; James 5:16; and 1 Peter 3:3-4
THE POINT: Guys and girls can be good friends.

Relationships as a Core Christian Belief

Nothing in the world brings a smile to young people as quickly as seeing the face of someone they love. Conversely, nothing hurts quite as deeply as losing that love when people leave or relationships fail. So kids are faced with a constant struggle. Since relationships can be a powerful source of pleasure and happiness, all young people want and need them. However, because those same relationships can fail and produce broken hearts and bitter tears, kids sometimes avoid them or enter into them only halfheartedly. Nevertheless, one fact remains: Your kids need relationships. They need intimacy, vulnerability, trust, acceptance, challenge—all the qualities that only close relationships can bring.

One very important relationship in the lives of young people is **friendship**. The first study in the book will help kids see both the responsibility and the joy that come with solid friendships. Kids will be encouraged to support their friends through love, encouragement, and service.

The second study in this book addresses the very real problem of **gangs**. In this study, kids will examine the types of "friendships" that exist within gangs and compare those to true friendships. Through this experience, teenagers will discover that people who are real friends always encourage others to achieve a higher model of living.

Competition within relationships can be a problem for kids as they struggle to live according to God's standards rather than the world's standards. The third study will help kids to understand that God's opinion of them is the only one that really matters; if they strive to live their lives according to God's plan, their relationships will be healthy and lasting.

The fourth study in this series will help kids examine **dating** issues. Through this study, kids will discover God's plan for their dating relationships, and they will see that such relationships are best when they're built on a strong foundation of friendship.

Young people need someone to show them how to develop healthy and lasting relationships. By using the studies within this Core Christian Belief, you'll be able to teach and model for them biblical principles for forming good relationships with others.

For a more comprehensive look at this Core Christian Belief, read Group's ***Get Real: Making Core Christian Beliefs Relevant to Teenagers.***

DEPTHFINDER
WHAT THE BIBLE TEACHES ABOUT RELATIONSHIPS

To help you effectively guide your kids toward this Core Christian Belief, use these overviews as a launching point for a more in-depth study of relationships.

- **God wants us to live in relationship with others.** God didn't create us to live alone. We're social beings. Our most important relationship is with God, but we also need significant relationships with other people to enjoy life as God intended (Genesis 2:18; Deuteronomy 6:4-5; Ecclesiastes 4:9-12; Song of Solomon 8:6-7; and 1 Corinthians 12:20-21).

- **God established a variety of human relationships.** Since people are different, their relationship needs will be different. Even a person's individual needs will be different during the various stages of his or her life. Still, people generally need a variety of relationships with family, friends, co-workers, and neighbors (Leviticus 19:18, 33-34; Proverbs 17:17; 18:22, 24; 1 Corinthians 7:1-7; and 2 Thessalonians 3:6-13).

- **Every relationship carries obligations.** Certain responsibilities go along with particular relationships. For example, parents should nurture their children, husbands and wives should remain faithful to each other, and employees and employers should treat each other fairly (Exodus 20:2-17; Matthew 7:9-11; Ephesians 5:21–6:9; and Philippians 2:3-4).

- **Because all people are equal before God, they should grant each other certain basic considerations.** The Bible instructs us to *love* everyone—including our enemies—as we love ourselves. We're to treat all people with *respect*, and allow those around us a reasonable amount of *freedom* to make their own choices. In addition, we're to be *honest* at all times and be willing to extend *forgiveness* to others because God has forgiven us (Genesis 1:26-27; Proverbs 12:17-22; 14:21; Matthew 6:14-15; Romans 14:1-12; Ephesians 4:25; and 1 Peter 2:17).

- **Christians should love, serve, and support one another.** God has created the body of Christ to be a community of Christians who share their lives with one another.

Consequently, we should come together regularly to worship God and minister to each other in humility, kindness, compassion, and encouragement (Acts 2:43-45; Romans 12:3-8; Galatians 5:13-14; Ephesians 4:11-16, 29-32; and Hebrews 10:23-25).
- **Christians should maintain positive relationships with non-Christians.** God doesn't want Christians to remove themselves from the world. Rather, we're to form relationships with non-Christians, show love to them, and tell about God's love for them in Jesus Christ. Our lives should draw non-Christians to God (Matthew 5:43-47; 28:18-20; Hebrews 12:14; James 1:27; and 1 Peter 2:11-12).
- **Conflict in relationships is inevitable.** Since we don't live in an ideal world, we'll experience the effects of damaged and broken relationships. The causes of conflict in relationships vary and include such things as misunderstanding, sin, and differing personalities (Genesis 3:14-19; Acts 15:36-41; 1 Corinthians 1:10-17; and Galatians 2:11-14).
- **It's important to resolve conflict.** When we experience conflict with someone, we should continue to grant that person the basic considerations due all people. We can try to resolve the conflict by discussing the problem one to one, offering a reasonable solution, or asking for the help of other Christians. In some instances, however, the only way to avoid ongoing conflict may be to break off relationship (Genesis 13:1-12; Proverbs 15:1; 17:9; Matthew 5:23-26; 18:15-35; 1 Corinthians 6:1-8; 7:12-16; and Titus 3:9-10).

CORE CHRISTIAN BELIEF OVERVIEW

Here are the twenty-four Core Christian Belief categories that form the backbone of Core Belief Bible Study Series:

The Nature of God	Jesus Christ	The Holy Spirit
Humanity	Evil	Suffering
Creation	The Spiritual Realm	The Bible
Salvation	Spiritual Growth	Personal Character
God's Justice	Sin & Forgiveness	The Last Days
Love	The Church	Worship
Authority	Prayer	Family
Service	Relationships	Sharing Faith

Look for Group's Core Belief Bible Study Series books in these other Core Christian Beliefs!

about

Bible Study Series
for junior high/middle school

Think for a moment about your young people. When your students walk out of your youth program after they graduate from junior high or high school, what do you want them to know? What foundation do you want them to have so they can make wise choices?

You probably want them to know the essentials of the Christian faith. You want them to base everything they do on the foundational truths of Christianity. Are you meeting this goal?

If you have any doubt that your kids will walk into adulthood knowing and living by the tenets of the Christian faith, then you've picked up the right book. All the books in Group's Core Belief Bible Study Series encourage young people to discover the essentials of Christianity and to put those essentials into practice. Let us explain...

What Is Group's Core Belief Bible Study Series?

Group's Core Belief Bible Study Series is a biblically in-depth study series for junior high and senior high teenagers. This Bible study series utilizes four defining commitments to create each study. These "plumb lines" provide structure and continuity for every activity, study, project, and discussion. They are:

- **A Commitment to Biblical Depth**—Core Belief Bible Study Series is founded on the belief that kids not only *can* understand the deeper truths of the Bible but also *want* to understand them. Therefore, the activities and studies in this series strive to explain the "why" behind every truth we explore. That way, kids learn principles, not just rules.

- **A Commitment to Relevance**—Most kids aren't interested in abstract theories or doctrines about the universe. They want to know how to live successfully right now, today, in the heat of problems they can't ignore. Because of this, each study connects a real-life need with biblical principles that speak directly to that need. This study series finally bridges the gap between Bible truths and the real-world issues kids face.

- **A Commitment to Variety**—Today's young people have been raised in a sound bite world. They demand variety. For that reason, no two meetings in this study series are shaped exactly the same.

- **A Commitment to Active and Interactive Learning**—Active learning is learning by doing. Interactive learning simply takes active learning a step further by having kids teach each other what they've learned. It's a process that helps kids internalize and remember their discoveries.

For a more detailed description of these concepts, see the section titled "Why Active and Interactive Learning Works With Teenagers" beginning on page 55.

So how can you accomplish all this in a set of four easy-to-lead Bible studies? By weaving together various "power" elements to produce a fun experience that leaves kids challenged and encouraged.

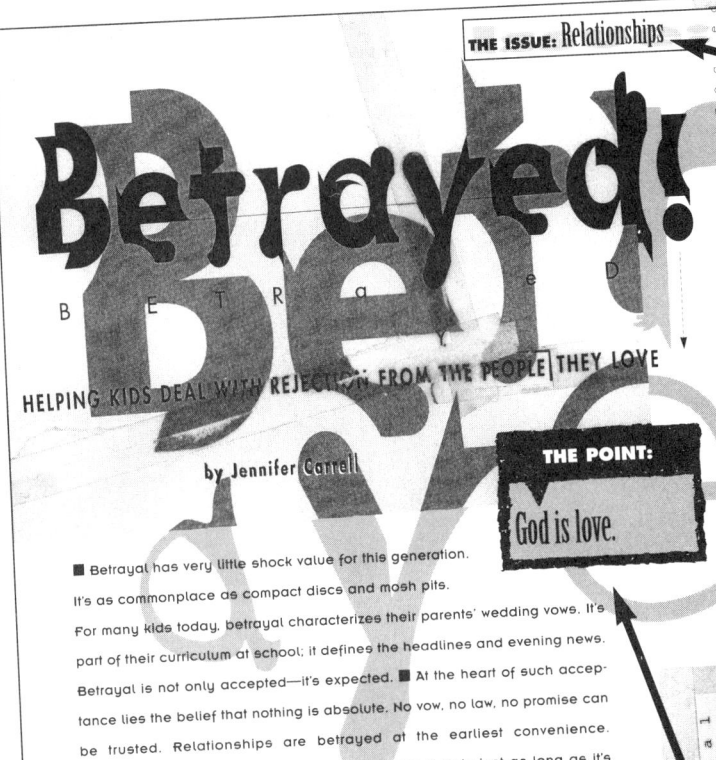

- **A Relevant Topic**—More than ever before, kids live in the now. What matters to them and what attracts their hearts is what's happening in their world at this moment. For this reason, every Core Belief Bible Study focuses on a particular hot topic that kids care about.

- **A Core Christian Belief**—Group's Core Belief Bible Study Series organizes the wealth of Christian truth and experience into twenty-four Core Christian Belief categories. These twenty-four headings act as umbrellas for a collection of detailed beliefs that define Christianity and set it apart from the world and every other religion. Each book in this series features one Core Christian Belief with lessons suited for junior high or senior high students.

  "But," you ask, "won't my kids be bored talking about all these spiritual beliefs?" No way! As a youth leader, you know the value of using hot topics to connect with young people. Ultimately teenagers talk about issues because they're searching for meaning in their lives. They want to find the one equation that will make sense of all the confusing events happening around them. Each Core Belief Bible Study answers that need by connecting a hot topic with a powerful Christian principle. Kids walk away from the study with something more solid than just the shifting ebb and flow of their own opinions. They walk away with a deeper understanding of their Christian faith.

- **The Point**—This simple statement is designed to be the intersection between the Core Christian Belief and the hot topic. Everything in the study ultimately focuses on The Point so that kids study it and allow it time to sink into their hearts.

- **The Study at a Glance**—A quick look at this chart will tell you what kids will do, how long it will take them to do it, and what supplies you'll need to get it done.

Helpful Stuff   11

- **The Bible Connection**—This is the power base of each study. Whether it's just one verse or several chapters, The Bible Connection provides the vital link between kids' minds and their hearts. The content of each Core Belief Bible Study reflects the belief that the true power of God—the power to expose, heal, and change kids' lives—is contained in his Word.

- **Depthfinder Boxes**— These informative sidelights located throughout each study add insight into a particular passage, word, historical fact, or Christian doctrine. Depthfinder boxes also provide insight into teen culture, adolescent development, current events, and philosophy.

- **Leader Tips**— These handy information boxes coach you through the study, offering helpful suggestions on everything from altering activities for different-sized groups to streamlining discussions to using effective discipline techniques.

- **Handouts**—Most Core Belief Bible Studies include photocopiable handouts to use with your group. Handouts might take the form of a fun game, a lively discussion starter, or a challenging study page for kids to take home—anything to make your study more meaningful and effective.

Helpful Stuff   12

The Last Word on Core Belief Bible Studies

Soon after you begin to use Group's Core Belief Bible Study Series, you'll see signs of real growth in your group members. Your kids will gain a deeper understanding of the Bible and of their own Christian faith. They'll see more clearly how a relationship with Jesus affects their daily lives. And they'll grow closer to God.

But that's not all. You'll also see kids grow closer to one another.

That's because this series is founded on the principle that Christian faith grows best in the context of relationship. Each study uses a variety of interactive pairs and small groups and always includes discussion questions that promote deeper relationships. The friendships kids will build through this study series will enable them to grow *together* toward a deeper relationship with God.

THE ISSUE: Friendship

Lean on Me

Helping Kids Be Better Friends

BY CINDY S. HANSEN

■ Most of us remember the commercial. An elderly lady lies on the floor and yells for medical assistance, "Help! I've fallen and I can't get up!" It's become a cultural joke, but it illustrates an important point—we all need friends who'll help us when we fall. ■ Junior high isn't an easy time—you remember it. Kids tearing each other down. Voices changing. Parents enforcing strict rules. And in today's world, it's even tougher. Some kids return to lonely, empty houses after school. Others struggle with the temptations of drugs, sex, and gangs. More than ever before, kids need committed friends who care enough to help them through their struggles. ■ This study explores how friends commit to helping each other through hard times.

THE POINT:

Friends commit to helping each other.

The Study AT A GLANCE

SECTION	MINUTES	WHAT STUDENTS WILL DO	SUPPLIES
Learning Games	10 to 15	LEAN ON ME, FRIENDS—Form a supportive circle and discuss what it's like to lean on friends when in need.	
	5 to 10	TRUST ME TO HELP—Race around obstacles in pairs with one partner helping the other.	Masking tape
Bible Investigation	5 to 10	BACKGROUND CHECK—Learn background facts about Jonathan and David.	Bibles
	10 to 15	A FRIEND IN NEED—Discover how Jonathan helped David and teach each other qualities of good friends.	Bibles, "Good Friends" Depthfinder (p. 22)
	5 to 10	SWEET FRIENDSHIP—Drink unsweetened and sweetened lemonade.	Pitcher, lemon juice, water, sugar, spoon, cups, paper, pencils
Reflection	up to 5	COMMITMENT CIRCLE—Work together to lift one person.	Bibles

notes:

THE POINT OF "LEAN ON ME":

Friends commit to helping each other.

THE BIBLE CONNECTION

1 SAMUEL 18:1-4; 20:1-42 These passages describe David and Jonathan's committed friendship.

In this study, kids will celebrate friendship. They'll discover ways to be committed, helping friends through a variety of fun experiences and an exploration of Jonathan and David's friendship.

Through this friendship celebration, kids can discover that friends commit to helping each other through difficult times.

Explore the verses in The Bible Connection; then examine the information in the Depthfinder boxes throughout the study to gain a deeper understanding of how these Scriptures connect with your young people.

THE STUDY

LEARNING GAMES ▼

Lean on Me, Friends (10 to 15 minutes)
Say: **Friends are an important part of our lives. Today we're going to celebrate our friendships and discover ways friends commit to helping each other. Good friends can lean on each other for support during hard times. Let me show you what I mean.**

Have students form a circle, stand with their feet shoulder-width apart, and join hands with the people on both sides of them. Then have kids step back until they feel some "pull" between each other. Have kids number off by twos. Say: **When I say, "Lean on me, friends," all "ones" will lean toward the center of the circle and all "twos" will lean away. Keep your bodies stiff—don't bend at**

LEADER TIP for Lean on Me, Friends

If kids don't take this activity seriously, have them sit down to discuss these questions:
● What's it like to try this activity without everyone cooperating?
● How is this like when you need a friend to support you and your friend lets you down?
Say: To make this activity work, we all need to commit to helping each other. Will you do that? If kids are willing to commit to the activity, try the circle activity again. If they're not willing, move to the next activity.

Lean on Me   17

LEADER TIP for The Study

Whenever you tell groups to discuss a list of questions, write the questions on newsprint, and tape the newsprint to the wall so groups can answer the questions at their own pace.

the waist! **We'll try to support each other in this position for ten seconds. We'll practice once and then try it again. Ready? Lean on me, friends!**

(If you have fewer than eight kids in your class, vary the activity by having everyone hold hands and lean away from the center of the circle.)

Practice once or twice until everyone can hold the position for at least ten seconds. Then have kids hold the position while you pray: **Dear God, thanks for all these fun friends. Teach us how to commit to helping our friends during tough times in life. Thanks, God, for being the best friend we could ever have. Amen.**

Have kids form pairs to discuss these questions:

● **What were you thinking and feeling as you leaned on the group?**

● **How was our circle like leaning on someone during a difficult time?**

● **How have you leaned on a friend in the past? How did that feel?**

● **How has a friend leaned on you? How did that feel?**

● **How does leaning on each other affect your friendship?**

Invite kids to share their answers with the larger group. Then say: **True friends let us lean on them during tough times. <u>Friends commit to helping each other</u>. In the next activity, we'll practice helping our friends.**

LEADER TIP for Trust Me to Help

Keep the masking tape pieces from sticking to you by lightly licking your fingers before you lay each piece on the floor. Then touch the pieces around the edges only.

Trust Me to Help (5 to 10 minutes)

Say: **We're going to help each other create and run an obstacle course.**

Have kids work together to place obstacles such as chairs, tables, boxes, and books around the room. Then hand each student a yard-long strip of masking tape. Have kids help you place one-inch bits of masking tape all over the floor, sticky side up, about six inches apart from each other. Make sure the obstacles and tape are evenly distributed in the room.

Have kids stand on one side of the room with their partners from the

---

DEPTH FINDER — UNDERSTANDING THE BIBLE

In John 15:12-13, Jesus said, "This is my command: Love each other as I have loved you. The greatest love a person can show is to die for his friends."

Your kids may never have to die for their friends, but they can love their friends by making other sacrifices. When they've committed to a friend who needs help, your students may need to sacrifice time that they would have spent doing homework, going to a movie, or even sleeping. By giving up something they want or need, your kids "die" for their friends.

When you notice your students fulfilling their commitments to help their friends, affirm them for following Jesus' command.

previous activity. Say: **We're going to help each other run this race. Choose one person in your pair to be the Helping Friend and the other to be the Trusting Friend.**

When pairs have done this, say: **We're going to run a race across the room around the obstacles and tape. The object is to have the fewest bits of tape on your shoes at the end of the race.**

Trusting Friends, close your eyes and trust your Helping Friends to coach you across the room. Helping Friends, guide your Trusting Friends to the other side, making sure your partner steers clear of all obstacles and tape. You may not touch your partner. When you reach the opposite side of the room, sit down. Ready? Go!

(If you have a small room, have half the class go first while the other half watches the action. When the first half has finished, lay down more bits of masking tape, and have the rest of the pairs run the race.)

When all pairs have finished the race, count the bits of tape stuck to the bottom of everyone's shoes.

Have pairs discuss the following questions:
● **What did you do to make it through the maze of obstacles and tape on the floor?**
● **What things in real life are like the obstacles and tape in this game?**
● **What was it like to be a Trusting Friend during this activity?**
● **How's this like real life when you trust someone to help you during hard times?**
● **What was it like to be a Helping Friend?**
● **How's this like helping a friend during hard times?**

Invite kids to share their answers with the whole class. Then say: **In real life, we have chances to help and trust our friends through sticky situations. <u>Friends commit to helping each other.</u>**

Have kids move the obstacles back to their original positions and pick up any leftover tape.

BIBLE INVESTIGATION ▼

Background Check (5 to 10 minutes)
Say: **We're going to learn about a pair of Old Testament friends who were committed to helping each other—David and Jonathan. Before we learn about their friendship, let's run a quick background check on them.**

Have kids stay with their partners. Say: **In a moment I'll assign you and your partner a Bible passage that tells a background fact about David or Jonathan. Read the passage together, and help each other discover the fact. Then come up with one sentence that expresses that fact.**

Assign each pair one of the passages listed in the "Background Check" Depthfinder (p. 20). If you have fewer than sixteen students in your class, assign two or more passages to some pairs. If you have more

LEADER TIP for The Study

Kids will form pairs during "Lean on Me, Friends" and stay in the same pairs for the rest of the study. You may want to encourage your students to pair up either with good friends or with people they don't know well. Here are advantages and disadvantages to both approaches.

● **If you allow your kids to choose good friends,** they'll probably be more willing to share deeply during discussions. They also may immediately apply this study by committing to help each other through tough times. However, not everyone will have a good friend in class.

● **If you encourage kids to form pairs with people they don't know well,** they might develop new friendships. Students may also feel freer to talk about how they can commit to their good friends, and these new friends can keep each other accountable to their commitments. This approach also benefits your class as a whole as kids get to know people outside their normal circle of friends. However, kids are less likely to share deeply with people they don't know well.

Lean on Me 19

Leader TIP for The Study

Because this topic can be so powerful and relevant to kids' lives, your group members may be tempted to get caught up in the issues and lose sight of the deeper biblical principle found in The Point. Help your kids grasp The Point by guiding kids' focus to the biblical investigation and discussing how God's truth connects with reality in their lives.

DEPTHFINDER — BACKGROUND CHECK

Your students will better understand the intensity of Jonathan and David's friendship when they know more about Jonathan's and David's lives. Here's a quick background check on them.

1. **1 Samuel 13:1, 16**—Jonathan was King Saul's son.
2. **1 Samuel 16:1, 11-13**—David was a shepherd boy. His dad's name was Jesse. God, through the prophet Samuel, chose David as the next king of Israel.
3. **1 Samuel 17:48-50**—David used a sling to kill Goliath, the giant.
4. **1 Samuel 18:1**—David and Jonathan were best friends.
5. **1 Samuel 18:6-9**—King Saul was jealous of David.
6. **1 Samuel 20:12-13**—Jonathan helped David escape when King Saul wanted to kill David.
7. **2 Samuel 1:4**—Jonathan and King Saul died in battle.
8. **2 Samuel 5:4**—David became king.

than sixteen students, assign the same passages to two or more pairs.

When pairs have finished, say: **Let's complete our background check on Jonathan and David by sharing the facts we just learned. When I point to your pair, stand up, say your sentence together, then sit down. Then I'll point to the next pair. We'll do this until we've checked out all the facts about David's and Jonathan's backgrounds.**

Point to the pair who read the first passage and proceed with the background check.

Say: **Now that we've learned about Jonathan's and David's backgrounds, let's explore their friendship and how they committed to helping each other.**

A Friend in Need (10 to 15 minutes)

Before the study, photocopy the "Good Friends" Depthfinder (p. 22), making one copy for every two students. Highlight a different section on each copy. If you have fewer than sixteen students, highlight two or more sections on each copy. If you have more than sixteen students, highlight the same sections on two or more copies.

Hand one highlighted copy of the "Good Friends" Depthfinder to each pair. Then say: **Study the Bible passage and the information highlighted on the handout I gave you. Then think of a creative, dramatic way to teach what you learned to the rest of the class. For example, you could tell the information like TV newscasters, then "cut to the scene of the action" and act out the Bible passage.**

When students are ready, have each pair teach the rest of the class what it learned about Jonathan and David. Then have pairs discuss these questions:

● **When have you been a helping friend like Jonathan?**
● **When has someone been a helping friend to you?**
● **From David and Jonathan's example, what's one thing you want to remember about being a helping friend?**

Lean on Me 20

● **What's one way you can help a friend in the coming week?**

Say: <u>Friends commit to helping each other</u>. Jonathan helped David run from King Saul when David's life was in danger. Jonathan and David were committed, helping friends, and we can learn from their friendship. Let's think of ways we can help our friends.

Sweet Friendship (5 to 10 minutes)

You'll need a two-quart pitcher filled with one cup lemon juice and six and one-half cups of water. You'll also need forty-eight small packets of sugar or twenty-four small packets of a sweetener such as Sweet'n Low. Don't stir the sugar into the lemon-juice mixture. (If you have more than ten students, double the recipe.)

Say: **When <u>friends commit to helping each other</u>, they add flavor to each other's life. Let's explore this right now.**

Pour a small amount of the unsweetened lemon-juice mixture into paper cups. Give kids each a cup, and have them sip from their cups at the same time. Ask:

● **How is this lemonade like life without helpful friends? like life without helping your friends?**

Give each pair paper and a pencil. Divide the packets of sugar equally among all the pairs. If you can't divide all the packets equally, give each pair the same number of packets and keep the remaining packets with you.

Say: **Our lives can be bitter and lonely without the supportive help of friends. But with the help of kind friends, life can be sweet and good. In your pairs, think of specific ways friends can commit to helping each other. Write one way for each packet of sugar. For example, friends could pray for each other every day, call each other on the telephone, and encourage each other.**

When kids are ready, have pairs explain their ideas. For each idea, have them pour a packet of sugar in the pitcher. After all pairs have had a turn, pour any remaining sugar packets into the lemonade, mix the sugar and lemonade, and pour the mixture into new cups.

Have kids each serve a cup of sweetened lemonade to their partners and say how their partners make friendship sweet. For example, "You make friendship sweet because you listen to me." Have all friends toast each other then drink the lemonade.

Say: **Just as all of you made this lemonade sweet by adding sugar to it, you all make life sweet when you help your friends.**

REFLECTION ▼

Commitment Circle (up to 5 minutes)

Say: **Throughout today's study, we've learned that <u>friends commit to helping each other</u>. Let's reflect on this one last time before we leave.**

LEADER TIP for Commitment Circle

If your students clown around and drop your volunteer, ask the group these questions:
- What was it like to let somebody down in this activity?
- What was it like to be let down in this activity?
- How is this experience like real life when you break a commitment to help a friend? when someone breaks his or her commitment to help you?
- How does breaking your commitment to help affect your relationship?

After this discussion, ask the volunteer if he or she is willing to allow the group to try again. If the volunteer agrees, ask the others if they'll commit to supporting the volunteer. Allow the kids to try again only if they make the commitment. If the volunteer is unwilling to allow the group to lift him or her, say: **It's understandable that [name] doesn't trust the group right now. Sometimes when we break our commitments, we have to earn our friends' trust again.**

Say: **In a minute we're going to physically support one of you. We'll form a circle and support a volunteer with our arms. As we do this, remember that <u>friends commit to helping each other</u>.** Everyone in this circle must commit to supporting our volunteer, because if we drop this person, he or she could get hurt. So be careful and pay attention as we do this activity.

Have one student volunteer stand near you, and hand that person a Bible. Then have the rest of the group form a circle. Say: **Everyone in the circle, reach out your right hand and clasp the right hand of someone across from you. Now, reach out your left hand and clasp the left hand of the same person.** If you have an uneven number of kids in the circle, join in this activity.

When everyone has clasped hands, say: **Everyone bend your knees and keep your hands clasped.** Have the volunteer lie down in the center of the circle on the clasped hands and arms. Say: **Now let's lift and support** [name].

Have the supported person read aloud Ecclesiastes 4:9-10. Then say: **Two are better than one. Our friendships make us strong.**

Have kids let the volunteer down then support other volunteers if there's time.

DEPTHFINDER — GOOD FRIENDS

Here are some qualities of good friends that we can learn from Jonathan and David.

1. **Good friends love each other (1 Samuel 18:1-4).** David and Jonathan loved each other and committed to being friends.

2. **Good friends can ask each other for help (1 Samuel 20:1-4).** David asked Jonathan why Saul, Jonathan's dad, had tried to kill David.

3. **Good friends commit to helping each other (1 Samuel 20:5-13).** Jonathan agreed to help David discover how Saul really felt about David.

4. **Good friends share mutual faith in God (1 Samuel 20:12-17).** In the presence of God, Jonathan and David promised not to let Saul's feelings about David ruin their friendship.

5. **Good friends remain faithful through tough times (1 Samuel 20:18-23).** Jonathan and David planned a signal to communicate whether Saul wanted to kill David. Jonathan loyally protected David when his life was in danger.

6. **Good friends stick up for each other (1 Samuel 20:24-34).** Jonathan made an excuse for David's absence from the feast. Saul was so angry that he tried to kill Jonathan.

7. **Good friends follow through on commitments (1 Samuel 20:35-40).** Jonathan followed through on his commitment to communicate to David whether Saul wanted to kill him.

8. **Good friends show affection and appreciation (1 Samuel 20:41-42).** Jonathan and David embraced and recommitted themselves to each other before parting ways.

Permission to photocopy this Depthfinder from Group's Core Belief Bible Study Series granted for local church use. Copyright © Group Publishing, Inc., P.O. Box 481, Loveland, CO 80539.

Have everyone unclasp hands and sit down. Say: **I challenge you to commit to helping a friend in a specific way this week. Think of one way you could help a friend who's facing a tough time. Maybe you could help a friend study for a test. Maybe you could listen to a friend whose parents are in the middle of a divorce.**

Allow kids a moment to think of ways they can help hurting friends. Have kids meet with their original partners to share their helping ideas and pray for each other to follow through with their commitments. Have partners exchange phone numbers so that they can call and remind each other of their commitments.

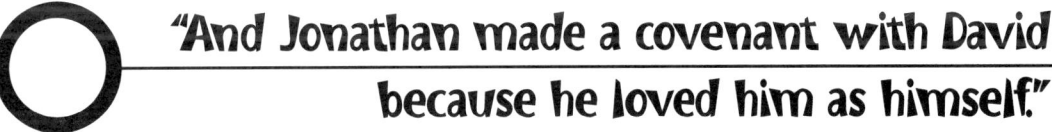

"And Jonathan made a covenant with David because he loved him as himself."

—1 Samuel 18:3

THE ISSUE: Gangs

"I Would Die For You"

Why Kids Stay in Gangs

by Lisa Baba Lauffer

■ Put yourself in your kids' shoes. ■ Allow a gang to beat, bloody, and bruise you as an initiation rite, and you earn the loyalty of a group of kids who say they'd give their lives for you. It seems a small price to pay for such enduring friendship. ■ But is it really friendship? Gangs may give you their loyalty, but they expect yours in return—loyalty in conforming to their creeds, to their way of dressing, to their way of life. Loyalty that says you'd die for them, too. And not just the "romantic" death of defending a friend until the end. Death of your individuality. Death of your morality. Death of your body by random, senseless violence. ■ This is friendship?

■ This study explores the difference between gangs and other groups of friends—to help kids see the difference between true friends who inspire excellence and false friends who drag them down.

THE POINT:

True friends inspire excellence.

The Study
AT A GLANCE

SECTION	MINUTES	WHAT STUDENTS WILL DO	SUPPLIES
Creative Brainstorm	5 to 10	THE TRUE MEASURE OF FRIENDSHIP—Create a yardstick to measure whether people are true or false friends.	Bibles, newsprint, markers, index cards, yarn, tape
Evaluation	25 to 30	GANG STUDY—Study stories of gangs today and "gangs" in the Bible and measure them against the "friendship yardstick."	Bibles, "Gang Stories" handout (p. 33), construction paper, masking tape, paper plates, rubber bands, plastic trash bags, twist ties, newsprint, chalk, toilet paper, glue, foil, folding chairs
Bible Comparison	10 to 15	A TASTE OF FRIENDSHIP—Study the difference between gangs and the body of Christ.	Bibles, unsweetened chocolate, "Gang or Body of Christ?" Depthfinder (p. 30)
Quiet Time	up to 5	MY FRIENDS—Spend time alone evaluating their friendships.	Paper, pencils
Inspiration Time	up to 5	BACK UP—Write a true-friend quality for other group members.	Index cards, pencils

notes:

THE POINT OF "I WOULD DIE FOR YOU":

True friends inspire excellence.

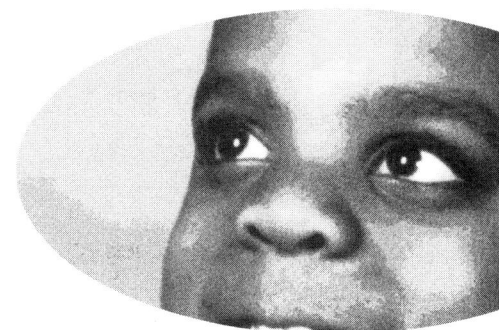

THE BIBLE CONNECTION

GENESIS 37:18-35; 1 SAMUEL 22:1-2; 24:3-7; and NEHEMIAH 4:7-23	Groups of friends in the Bible either inspire excellence in each other or drag each other down.
JOHN 15:12-17	Jesus states that the greatest love anyone can have is to die for his or her friends.

In this study, kids will create a standard for determining true friends. To this standard, they'll compare gangs in real life and groups in the Bible and then evaluate their own relationships.

Through this comparison, kids can discover that true friends encourage each other to meet their full potential.

Explore the verses in The Bible Connection; then study the information in the Depthfinder boxes throughout the study to gain a deeper understanding of how these Scriptures connect with your young people.

BEFORE THE STUDY

For "The True Measure of Friendship" activity, write "True Friends" in bold letters on one sheet of newsprint and "False Friends" on another sheet of newsprint. Tape the signs to the floor at opposite ends of your meeting room. Connect the signs by stringing a length of yarn between them. Tape the yarn to the floor.

LEADER TIP for The Study

Because this topic can be so powerful and relevant to kids' lives, your group members may be tempted to get caught up in the issues and lose sight of the deeper biblical principle found in The Point. Help your kids grasp The Point by guiding kids' focus to the biblical investigation and discussing how God's truth connects with reality in their lives.

"I Would Die for You" 27

THE STUDY

LEADER TIP for The Study

Whenever you tell groups to discuss a list of questions, write the questions on newsprint, and tape the newsprint to the wall so groups can answer the questions at their own pace.

CREATIVE BRAINSTORM ▼

The True Measure of Friendship (5 to 10 minutes)

When kids arrive, say: **Today we're going to discuss friendship. To measure whether someone is a true or false friend, let's create a "friendship yardstick." First, let's define the end points of our yardstick.**

Have kids form trios. Give each trio six index cards and a marker. Say: **In your trios, brainstorm three characteristics of false friends. For example, you might think that someone is a false friend if he or she lies to you. When you've thought of three false-friend characteristics, write each one on a separate card. So for our example, you could write "lies to you" on one of your cards.**

When trios have finished, have them each share with the rest of the class one false-friend characteristic they've identified. Continue the rounds of sharing if trios have false-friend characteristics that still haven't been mentioned.

Point to the signs you prepared before the study. Then say: **We're going to tape the cards with the false-friend characteristics to the "False Friends" end of our yardstick. However, we can only include half of the false-friend characteristics we brainstormed. So we need to decide which of those characteristics best describe a false friend.**

Have students debate and negotiate among themselves to decide which characteristics should be taped to the "False Friends" sign. When they've chosen half of the original false-friend characteristics, tape those cards to the sign.

Say: **Now in your trios brainstorm three characteristics of true friends. Do the same thing you did with false friends, but before you begin, read John 15:12-17.**

While trios read the passage and brainstorm characteristics of true friends, write "inspire excellence" on one index card.

Have trios share their true-friend characteristics with the class in the same way as before. Then have students debate which cards to tape to the "True Friends" end of the yardstick, allowing them to include only half of the cards.

LEADER TIP for The True Measure of Friendship

If your kids have already said that true friends inspire excellence, don't add your "inspire excellence" card to the list. Instead, point to their card as you say, "True friends inspire excellence."

Have trios discuss these questions:
● **What was your reaction to debating which false- and true-friend characteristics to include on our friendship yardstick?**
● **How is deciding which characteristics to include on our yardstick like choosing friends?**

Say: **True friends inspire excellence.** Tape your "inspire excellence" card to the "True Friends" sign. Ask:
● **What does "excellence" mean to you?**

"I Would Die for You" 28

Say: **When we say that <u>true friends inspire excellence</u>, we mean that true friends want what's best for us. They want us to grow into the best people we can be.**

EVALUATION ▼

Gang Study (25 to 30 minutes)

Say: **When we choose friends, we need to figure out who will help us be our best and who will drag us down. We're going to take a quick look at gangs today to see what types of relationships are involved in gangs.**

Assign each trio either a story from the "Gang Stories" handout (p. 33) or one of the following Bible passages: Genesis 37:18-35 (Joseph's brothers); 1 Samuel 22:1-2 and 24:3-7 (David and his army); or Nehemiah 4:7-23 (Nehemiah and the Israelites who rebuilt Jerusalem's wall). Make sure you assign at least one gang story and one Scripture passage. If you have only one trio, have the trio read a gang story and a Scripture passage. If you have more than seven trios, give some trios duplicate gang stories or Bible passages.

Say: **As you read the story I've assigned you, think about the friendship it describes.**

While trios read, set out a variety of items such as construction paper, masking tape, paper plates, rubber bands, plastic trash bags, twist ties, newsprint, chalk, toilet paper, glue, foil, and folding chairs. The more items you gather, the more creative your kids can be.

When trios have finished, say: **Using the materials I've provided, create a sculpture about the kind of "gang" friendship described in your stories. For example, you could join four trash bags together with one rubber band to represent a group of friends who stay together through tough situations.**

Have trios create their sculptures. Then ask:

● **How does your sculpture represent the "gang" friendship you read about?**

● **Where does the gang in your story belong on the friendship yardstick? Place your sculpture (or prop) on the friendship yardstick in the appropriate place on or between False Friends and**

DEPTH FINDER — UNDERSTANDING THESE KIDS

Though gang members come from a variety of backgrounds, they seem to have one thing in common: chaotic family life. In the midst of the chaos, many basic emotional and physical needs of kids go unmet. To meet their need for validation, affection, belonging, and security, kids turn to gangs. Many gang members acknowledge that if they found this sense of family, acceptance, and love elsewhere, they wouldn't have joined a gang.

LEADER TIP for Gang Study

If kids don't want to make a sculpture, have them create a skit instead, using the materials you provided as props. The trios can act out their assigned stories or create their own stories based on the qualities of friendship they read about.

When trios place their sculptures on the friendship yardstick, tell trios who performed skits to place a prop on the line.

True Friends now.
● Why did you place your sculpture where you did?

Have trios discuss these questions:
● Would you like to have the people in your story as friends? Why or why not?
● What would you do if you were already in a gang and you realized that it was a group of false friends?

Say: **Gang members may be true friends sometimes, but often they are not. True friends inspire excellence. We need to evaluate whether our groups of friends want what's best for us.**

BIBLE COMPARISON ▼

A Taste of Friendship (10 to 15 minutes)

Say: **I'm going to give each of you a piece of chocolate. Please wait until I've served everyone before you eat your piece.** When you've given everyone a piece of unsweetened chocolate, tell kids they can eat.

Have trios answer these questions:
● **What's the difference between the taste you expected and the actual taste?**
● **How is tasting this chocolate like joining a gang?**

Say: **When we need friends, we may look at a gang from the outside and think we want that type of friendship. But once we're in a gang, we may find it's different from what we expected.**

We're going to explore the difference between the friendship

DEPTHFINDER — GANG OR BODY OF CHRIST?

A Gang...
● puts a premium on conformity—dressing the same way, displaying the same color, doing what the gang wants you to do.
● brings out the worst in people. A crime one person wouldn't do alone, the whole group may do together without thinking twice.
● "jumps in" (fights) people who want to be members.
● claims that all members of the gang are like family.

The Body of Christ...
● celebrates differences. Each person brings unique attributes to the group to make it complete. (Read 1 Corinthians 12:4-7.)
● encourages each other to do good things. (Read Hebrews 10:24.)
● accepts all who believe Jesus saved them. (Read Romans 15:5-7.)
● believes that God is the Father, Jesus is a brother, and all believers are members of God's family. (Read Matthew 6:26; 12:48-50; Galatians 6:10; and Hebrews 2:11.)

Permission to photocopy this Depthfinder from Group's Core Belief Bible Study Series granted for local church use. Copyright © Group Publishing, Inc., P.O. Box 481, Loveland, CO 80539.

DEPTHFINDER: UNDERSTANDING THESE KIDS

"To join the Playgirl Gangsters, Regina had to fight two gang members at once for a count of sixty, ending up bloodied and bruised. In return, she got a new gang name, a tattoo, and a group of twenty or thirty girls willing, in theory at least, to kill and die for her."[1]

"The term 'wilding' refers to young people cruising in a pack, roaming the streets, and violently attacking passersby for 'fun.'"[2]

"We can't sugar-coat stuff...Jesus got beat down. People need to know what He went through for us...He did it willingly, knowing what He was doing because He loves all of us."[3]
Dove, Member of Gospel Gangstas, a Christian rap group

"Nicole had recently lost her father...Now she had turned to Nick [and had sex with him]. I knew I wasn't being a true friend if I didn't remind her what Jesus would think...She could either be thankful that I reminded her, and try to turn herself around, or she could get mad...But I had to take that risk. I couldn't be selfish about a friendship.'"[4]
Beth, Christian teenager

1. Gini Sikes, "Girls in the Hood," Scholastic Update (February 11, 1994). 2. Sandra Gardner, Street Gangs in America (1992). 3. Contemporary Christian Music (October, 1994). 4. Joe White, Over the Edge and Back (Sisters, Oregon: Questar Publishers, Inc., 1992).

gangs offer and the friendship you can find in the body of Christ. Give each trio a copy of the "Gang or Body of Christ?" Depthfinder (p. 30). Have trios read it then answer these questions:
● **Are you in a gang? Why or why not?**
● **How does your group of friends affect what you do?**
● **How do you choose your friends?**
● **Having discussed true friendship today, what's one thing you'll change about the way you choose friends?**

Say: <u>**True friends inspire excellence.**</u> Friendship is a free choice, not something we should just "let happen" to us. If we know that a gang will be like unsweetened chocolate, offering the appearance of friendship but not the genuine thing, we can avoid it. If we carefully choose our groups of friends, they can help us become the best we're meant to be.

QUIET TIME ▼

My Friends (up to 5 minutes)
Say: **Let's silently pray about the kinds of friends we have.**

Have kids scatter to spend this time alone. Say: **During this silent time, pray to God as you think about these questions:**

- How do I inspire excellence in my friends?
- Do I have true friends? Why or why not?
- What's one thing I can do to build friendships that inspire excellence?

Allow about forty seconds of silence between each question. After two minutes of silent time, give each student a piece of paper and a pencil. Say: **On your paper, create your own friendship yardstick. Write "False Friends" on the left side, "True Friends" on the right side, and connect them with a line. Then write your friends' initials on the line where you feel they belong—on one of the two ends or somewhere between the two.**

After one minute of silence, say: **Now write your name on the line where you feel you belong.**

Give students a few seconds to do this. Say: **On the bottom of your paper, write one way that you can become more of a true friend. And if you're in a group of false friends, write one way you can get yourself out of that group.**

Say: <u>True friends inspire excellence</u>, and we need to always evaluate whether our friendships help us and our friends help us be the best we can be.

INSPIRATION TIME ▼

Back Up (up to 5 minutes)

Have trio members sit with their backs together, facing outward. Give each person two index cards and one pencil. Say: **One way we can inspire excellence in others is by noticing their positive characteristics. Practice this now by writing words of encouragement for each of your trio members. Write each trio member's name on a separate card; then write one way that person is a true friend. For example, you may write, "Terry is a true friend because she accepts me even though we're different from each other."**

When kids have finished, have students each read what they wrote to their trio members. Then have kids tape their cards to the "True Friends" side of the friendship yardstick. Say: **You can all inspire excellence in your friends by affirming their positive qualities.**

As kids leave, challenge them to be true friends in the coming week by doing what they wrote about in the "My Friends" activity.

GANG Stories

An Eleven-Year-Old Killer
(A True Story)

Robert "Yummy" Sandifer, eleven, was on a mission. His gang had a score to keep, and Yummy got the orders: Fire on rival gang members. When he pulled the trigger of his 9 mm semiautomatic, the bullets sprayed into a crowd of kids, killing an innocent fourteen-year-old girl. With the police on his trail for the murder, Yummy desperately looked for a hiding place. Two of his "homies" said they'd found one for him and would take him to it.

Yummy's body was found lying in a railroad underpass, with two bullets to the back of his head. Yummy's "homies" are accused of the murder.

—Time magazine

Miss GTA
(A True Story)

They call her "Miss GTA," short for grand theft auto. Regina, nineteen, has earned the name by stealing numerous cars to sell for cash or just for joy riding. When her friends want the job done right, they know who to ask.

Regina's also proven her loyalty to her gang. At point-blank range, she shot a member of a rival gang in the heart as payback for the murder of a homegirl's younger brother. The police call the crime attempted murder, but Regina feels it was worth doing for a friend who's like family.

—Scholastic Update

The Big Time
(A True Story)

Two high school girls leave a party and head for home, but they never make it. On their way, they run into six male gang members. Fueled by alcohol and an adrenaline rush from "jumping in" two new members, all six gang members brutally assault and kill the girls. When accused of the murders, they show no remorse. Instead, they celebrate: "Hey, great! We've hit the big time!"

—Newsweek magazine

THE ISSUE: Competition

WINNER *Take All*

How Competition Can Hurt Your Relationships

by Jim Hawley

■ Three seconds left. Down by one. Coach calls the play. Ball comes to you. You fake left, drive around the right, and lay it up and in! No! It just bounces off the back rim. You lose. Your team loses. Your coach hangs his head. ■ Something like the above scenario happens to half of the teams in every game. The very nature of competition demands winners and losers. And while competition may have some benefits for young people, it also has some serious drawbacks—especially when kids get caught up in the intensity of competition and lose sight of the negative effects that competition may have on their relationships. ■ Use this study to help kids explore the effects of comparing themselves with others in their efforts to be winners.

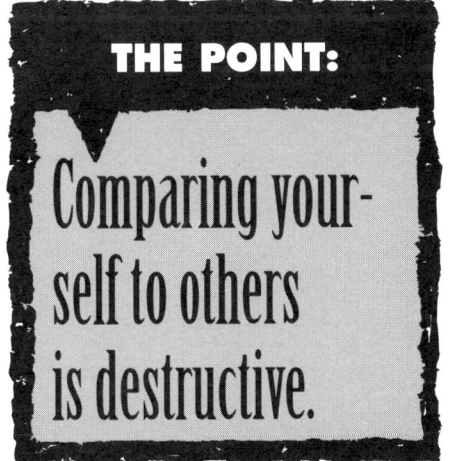

THE POINT:

Comparing yourself to others is destructive.

The Study AT A GLANCE

SECTION	MINUTES	WHAT STUDENTS WILL DO	SUPPLIES
Competitive Game 1	10 to 15	I LOSE, YOU LOSE—Compete in a game in which comparisons to each other result in everyone losing.	Balloons, markers
Personal Affirmation	5 to 10	WHAT I LIKE ABOUT ME—Create symbols of positive personal qualities and practice identifying those qualities.	Poster board, markers, tape
Bible Investigation	20 to 25	"BUT I WANT WHAT THEY'VE GOT!"—Explore various Bible characters' desire to have the qualities of others, see the problems it caused, then brainstorm positive ways to handle competition with others.	Bibles, "If Only I Were Like You!: Part 1" handout (p. 43), "If Only I Were Like You!: Part 2" handout (p. 44), newsprint, tape, markers
Competitive Game 2	10 to 15	I WIN, YOU WIN—Compete in a win-win game in which kids' individual qualities are affirmed.	Balloons, markers, masking tape

notes:

THE POINT OF "WINNER TAKE ALL":

Comparing yourself to others is destructive.

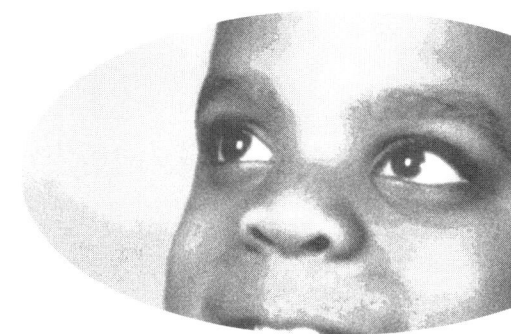

THE BIBLE CONNECTION

GENESIS 13:5-9; 1 SAMUEL 20:1-4, 12-17; and JOHN 3:22-30	These passages show three examples of people who handled competitive situations in healthy ways.
EXODUS 3:11-14; 4:10-16; 6:28–7:6; 12:50-51	God uses Moses and Aaron in the exodus from Egypt.
1 SAMUEL 1:3-11, 21-28; 2:19-21	Hannah responds to God's answer to her prayer for a son.
1 SAMUEL 18:5-9, 12-13; 19:1-10	Saul reacts to David's success.

In this study, kids will play a game in which they all lose because they can't have what others have. Then kids will affirm their good qualities before exploring the experiences of Bible people who struggled with wanting others' qualities. Finally, kids will play a game in which they all win.

Through these activities kids can discover that God has given each person special abilities and that recognizing those abilities will help them avoid comparing themselves to others.

Explore the verses in The Bible Connection; then examine the information in the Depthfinder boxes throughout the study to gain a deeper understanding of how these Scriptures connect with your young people.

LEADER TIP for The Study

Because this topic can be so powerful and relevant to kids' lives, your group members may be tempted to get caught up in issues and lose sight of the deeper biblical principle found in The Point. Help your kids grasp The Point by guiding kids to focus on the biblical investigation and discussing how God's truth connects with reality in their lives.

LEADER TIP for The Study

Whenever groups discuss a list of questions, write the questions on newsprint, and tape the newsprint to the wall so groups can discuss the questions at their own pace.

THE STUDY

COMPETITIVE GAME 1 ▼

I Lose, You Lose (10 to 15 minutes) Give each student several balloons and a marker. Have kids inflate their balloons and tie them off. Have kids think of several characteristics that are needed to be successful in a competitive career field such as professional sports, acting, or modeling. Have kids write those characteristics on the inflated balloons.

Put all the balloons in the middle of the room, and have kids play a game in which they all try to grab the balloon qualities they need to be successful in their chosen competitive careers. To prepare them for the game, explain these rules to the group:

1. Kids can select as many balloons as they can hold at one time.
2. Anyone can get another person's balloon simply by taking it.
3. The person holding *all* the balloon qualities when time is called is the winner.

Have kids play for two minutes; then call time. Debrief the game with the following questions:
● **What was playing this game like?**
● **Were you able to keep all the balloon qualities you needed? Why or why not?**
● **How is trying to collect the balloon qualities like trying to obtain these qualities in real life?**
● **How does it feel when you don't have that one competitive quality that you need or want?**

Say: **We've just experienced how <u>comparing yourself to others is destructive</u>.** Let's explore why this is true.

DEPTH FINDER — UNDERSTANDING THESE KIDS

Although some competition among teenagers is normal, psychologist David Elkind points out a unique type of unhealthy competition that also exists among teenagers. In his now classic text, *All Grown Up and No Place to Go*, Elkind explains that some teenagers who have low self-esteem and struggle with their attitudes, values, and habits are known as "patchwork self" personalities. Among kids with this type of personality, one common behavior is a supercompetitive nature. These competitive teenagers are overly concerned about grades, frequently cheat, and often become addicted to gambling.

As you lead this study, don't be afraid to talk openly with kids about the dangers of this kind of unhealthy competition. Point out that although competition is often unavoidable, they must learn to deal with it in positive ways.

Winner Take All 38

DEPTHFINDER: UNDERSTANDING THE TOPIC

Many kids will look to the Michael Jordans or Amy Grants of the world and unfairly compare themselves. It seems that all elite competitors—be they athletes or musicians or astronauts—share two things in common. First, they're especially gifted by God with a talent or skill in a particular area. Second, they have typically spent serious time and energy developing their gifts, skills, or abilities. Concert pianists often start playing in their preschool years. Most professional athletes have had success in their elementary years, leading to even more successful high school and college athletic experiences.

Many gifted or skilled persons fail to reach their goals for success simply because they fail to practice. And many more people fail to reach their goals because they lack the raw ability to be the best in a particular field. But we can each make the most of the abilities we do have and pursue goals that match our talents and our interests.

Encourage your kids to do the best with what they have and to measure success against their own potential, not the potential of others.

PERSONAL AFFIRMATION ▼

What I Like About Me (5 to 10 minutes)

Say: **It's easy to be frustrated because we don't have qualities we want. Let's focus on the qualities that we *do* like about ourselves. I'd like you to create a picture that symbolizes your best qualities.**

Give kids poster board and markers, and allow kids several minutes to draw their symbols. Then have kids tape their posters on the walls. Have kids form pairs.

Say: **Some of you may have drawn symbols that easily identify your positive qualities, while others' symbols may not be that clear in identifying those positive qualities. I want each pair to look up five different symbols (other than your own) and share with your partner what you think the symbols mean.**

When pairs finish, have them discuss these questions:
● **Was it easy or difficult to determine what qualities the symbols represent? Explain.**
● **How is that like or unlike the difficulty in recognizing the positive qualities in your own life?**

Say: **Sometimes it may be difficult to recognize your positive qualities, and so you believe you can only be successful if you have the qualities you see in others. This is not a new problem. Even some of those folks that we call Bible heroes had problems recognizing their own special qualities, and so they envied the abilities of others, which always got them into trouble. Next, see if you can discover more about why <u>comparing yourself to others is destructive</u>.**

BIBLE INVESTIGATION ▼

"But I Want What They've Got!" (20 to 25 minutes)

Have kids form three groups, and give each student an "If Only I Were Like You!: Part 1" handout (p. 43). Number groups from one to three, and have groups each study the handout section that corresponds to their assigned number. Give kids about ten minutes to study and discuss their group's situation. After ten minutes, have groups share some of their responses.

Then call everyone together, and ask groups to respond to these questions:

● **Why do you think your person wanted the abilities he or she saw in others?**

● **What would you tell this person about his or her abilities?**

● **Do you think this person's desire for another's ability was a good thing? Why or why not?**

Give each student an "If Only I Were Like You!: Part 2" handout (p. 44). Once again, have groups each study the handout section that corresponds to their assigned number. Give kids about eight minutes to study and discuss their group's situation. After eight minutes, have groups share some of their responses.

Then ask:

● **What are some other choices the people in your situation could have made?**

Say: **Let's look at more examples of handling competition in a healthy way.**

Give each group one of the following biblical situations. Have groups read the verses and watch for ways the people handled competition positively.

1. Abraham and Lot—Genesis 13:5-9
2. David and Jonathan—1 Samuel 20:1-4, 12-17
3. Jesus and John the Baptist—John 3:22-30

Give groups five minutes to read the verses and discuss how their assigned Bible characters handled competition positively. While kids work, tape a large sheet of newsprint to the wall. When groups are ready, have representatives from each group write some of their group's insights on the newsprint. Summarize by saying: **We've looked at several examples of people who struggled with competition. And now we've come up with a list of ways we can handle competition more positively in our own lives. As we've seen, <u>comparing yourself to others is destructive</u>. Let's revisit our earlier activity, but this time let's apply the principles we've learned.**

COMPETITIVE GAME 2 ▼

I Win, You Win (10 to 15 minutes)

Give each student a balloon. Have kids inflate their balloons and tie them off. Provide markers and long strips of masking tape, and have kids help each other tape their balloons to the front or back of their waists. Then say: **The object of this game is to write as many positive qualities about others as you can before time is up. When I say "go," I want you to think of a positive quality you see in some other person in this room. Write that positive quality on that person's balloon, initial what you wrote, and then repeat the process with another person in the room. The winner is the first person to sincerely write one quality on every person's balloon. Ready? Go!**

When you have a winner, congratulate him or her, and ask this person:

● **What was it like to write all the positive qualities for everyone?**

● **How is this game an example of a *good* form of competition?**

Then say: **When we look for positive qualities in others, we are all winners. Take a few minutes to write one or two more qualities on each person's balloon. Go!**

After kids have finished, have them remove their balloons and read

DEPTHFINDER — UNDERSTANDING THE BIBLE

Is competition sinful? Although the Bible is rich with imagery, illustrations, and stories relating to competition, determining whether competition is sinful is a difficult task. That's because Scripture at times seems to endorse competitive efforts, while at other times it clearly condemns them.

For example, in 1 Corinthians 12:12-26, Paul condemns competition within the church, since we are each unique before God and united as members of one body.

Likewise, when Jesus' disciples began arguing about which of them was the greatest, Jesus confronted them by saying, "If anyone wants to be first, he must be the very last, and the servant of all" (Mark 9:35). And so, these verses seem to indicate that competition is bad, especially within the church.

But wait! In 1 Corinthians 9:24-27 and again in 1 Timothy 2:5, Paul uses competitive imagery to illustrate the importance of commitment and dedication in the Christian life. Since Paul is using competition as a way to illustrate something that is good and desirable, it would seem that competition itself must also be good.

The truth is that competition does have benefits. It can develop focus and teach kids to be committed to a cause. It can build teamwork and increase self-confidence. It can also demonstrate the value of pursuing and achieving a goal through hard work and discipline.

But competition also has drawbacks. It can evoke envy, cause division among friends, and provoke people to embrace a false sense of pride about themselves or their importance compared with others.

So if your kids ask about whether competition is sinful, the best response might be to encourage them to evaluate their attitudes rather than the act of competing. If they're competing to improve themselves and develop skills that honor God, it's probably good. But if their goal is simply to defeat an opponent and try to prove that they are better than someone else, that is definitely bad and should be avoided.

the qualities written on them. Then have kids form pairs, and ask pairs to discuss these questions:

● **How did it feel to write a positive quality on someone else's balloon? Explain.**

● **How did it feel to have someone write a positive quality on your balloon? Explain.**

Read Matthew 20:25-28 aloud to your group. Ask:

● **How was Jesus' teaching in these verses demonstrated in our game?**

● **How can this passage help you when you start to compare your abilities with someone else's?**

Say: **We've looked at many ways <u>comparing yourself to others is destructive</u>. Let's take a moment to pray individually and thank God for the qualities written on our balloons, and any others we're thankful for, and to ask God to help us when we're tempted to compare ourselves to others.**

Take a minute to close in prayer.

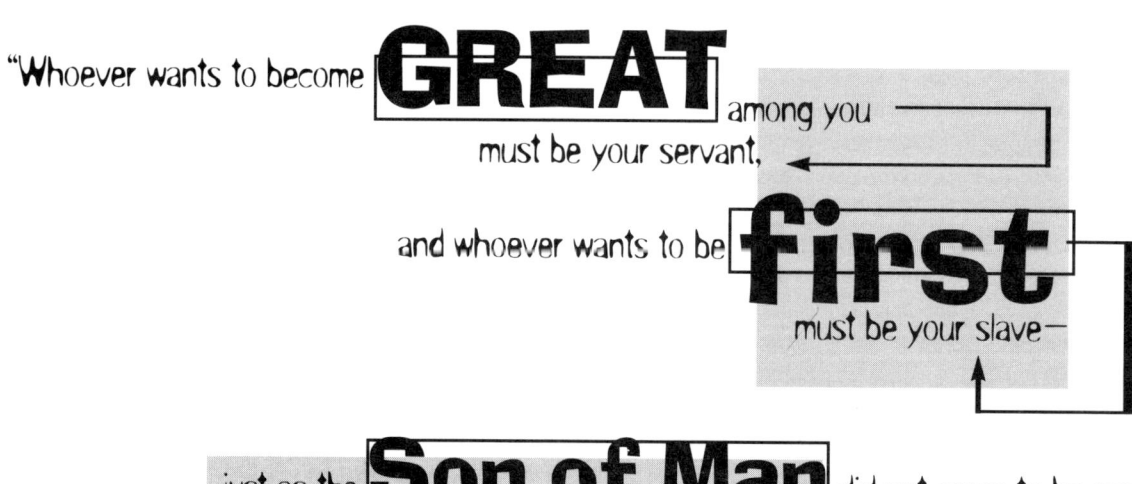

Part 1
"If Only I Were Like You!"

Read the descriptions and Scriptures related to your assigned person, and discuss in your group the questions listed at the bottom of the page.

1. Moses: *Wanting Speaking Ability*

God spoke to Moses through a burning bush and commissioned him to lead the people of Israel out of Egyptian slavery. But Moses didn't think he had the ability. Read Exodus 3:11-14; 4:10-16.

2. Saul: *Wanting Military Success*

Saul was the first king of Israel. David was his best military leader. But David's success made Saul jealous. Read 1 Samuel 18:5-9, 12-13.

3. Hannah: *Wanting Her Shame Vindicated*

Hannah was one of Elkanah's two wives. Her rival, Peninnah, had children, but Hannah had none. Read 1 Samuel 1:3-11.

Discussion Questions

- What did this person want that someone else had?

- How would you feel if you were in this person's place? Explain.

- When have you felt like this person in real life?

Permission to photocopy this handout from Group's Core Belief Bible Study Series granted for local church use. Copyright © Group Publishing, Inc., P.O. Box 481, Loveland, CO 80539.

Part 2
"If Only I Were Like You!"

Read the descriptions and Scriptures related to your assigned person to learn what happened next. Then discuss the questions listed at the bottom of the page.

1. Moses: *Teaming Up!*
God used Moses' leadership abilities along with Aaron's speaking ability to build a strong leader partnership. Read Exodus 6:28–7:6; 12:50-51.

2. Saul: *Refused to Accept His Weaknesses*
Saul was afraid that David would take his throne. Rather than face his own weaknesses, he tried to have David killed. Read 1 Samuel 19:1-10.

3. Hannah: *Offered Her Success to God*
Hannah gave birth to a son whom she named Samuel. She kept her promise by dedicating Samuel to the Lord. Read 1 Samuel 1:21-28; 2:19-21.

Discussion Questions

- How did this person use (or misuse) his or her abilities to deal with the situation?

- Based on this example, what's one way you can respond positively the next time you feel tempted to compare yourself with others?

THE ISSUE: Dating

Friendship First
Why Dating Should Focus on Friendship Before Romance

by Mikal Keefer

■ Dating—it's not for the weak of heart. It's expensive. Nerve-racking. Time-consuming. Often embarrassing. ■ But since dating guarantees a lifelong marriage with the perfect mate, it's worth every heart-stopping, nail-biting, anxiety-producing minute, right? ■ Umm...maybe not. Most dating relationships end in uncomfortable breakups and awkwardness. And of the marriages launched by dating, around half end in divorce. ■ The Bible says absolutely nothing about dating—it's a cultural phenomenon—but the Bible has *plenty* to say about relationships and marriage. ■ In this study your kids will compare dating with biblical mandates about building God-honoring relationships. The road to a healthy guy-girl relationship doesn't need to be littered with dating casualties. You'll help your teenagers avoid needless pain if you guide them in developing a critical skill they won't learn anywhere else: the skill of being *friends* with the opposite sex.

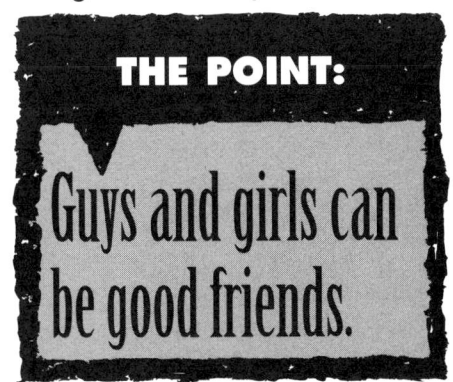

THE POINT:

Guys and girls can be good friends.

The Study AT A GLANCE

SECTION	MINUTES	WHAT STUDENTS WILL DO	SUPPLIES
Experiential Introduction	5 to 10	GIFT-WRAPPED GIZMOS—Open small gift bags, attempt to trade for a better gift, then compare the experience with dating.	Newspaper, tape, ribbons or bows, a dollar bill, gizmos from a junk drawer or workshop
Bible Exploration	20 to 25	THE IDEAL DATE—Identify characteristics of an ideal date then evaluate how to apply several Bible passages to dating relationships.	Bibles, plastic grocery bags, old magazines and newspapers, permanent markers, pens, "Focus on Friendship" handouts (pp. 53-54)
	10 to 15	WWW.ASKTHEEXPERTS.COM—Interview married couples to ask how friendship strengthens their relationships.	
Object Lesson Closing	10 to 15	MIRROR, MIRROR, IN MY HAND—Leave thumb prints on a mirror to demonstrate how dating relationships leave impressions on our lives.	Hand-held mirror

notes:

THE POINT OF "FRIENDSHIP FIRST":

Guys and girls can be good friends.

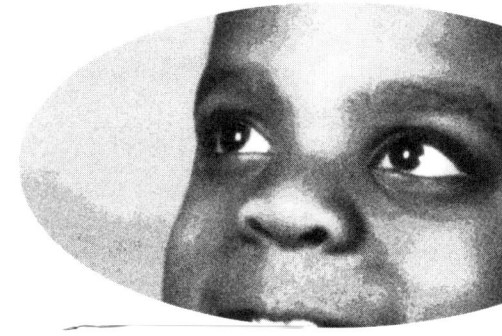

THE BIBLE CONNECTION

1 SAMUEL 16:7	Samuel explains that God doesn't look at outward appearances but values what's in the heart.
JOHN 13:34-35	Jesus teaches the importance of loving one another.
ROMANS 12:10, 16; 14:19	Paul explains how Christians should show love to one another.
PHILIPPIANS 1:9-10	Paul prays for our love for others to grow in knowledge and depth of insight.
1 TIMOTHY 5:2	Paul tells Timothy to treat older women as mothers and younger women as sisters.
JAMES 5:16	James tells Christians to confess their sins to one another.
1 PETER 3:3-4	Peter tells women to develop their inner beauty rather than focusing on their outward appearance.

In this study, kids will discover what the Bible says about guy-girl relationships, listen to what married couples say about being friends, and pray for the sort of impression they'll make on future dates.

Through this exploration, kids can recognize the value of friendship in their dating relationships and learn why it's important to focus on friendship first in *all* their peer relationships.

Explore the verses in The Bible Connection; then examine the information in the Depthfinder boxes throughout the study to gain a deeper understanding of how these Scriptures connect with your young people.

BEFORE THE STUDY

For the "Gift-Wrapped Gizmos" activity, gift-wrap a small package for every person in your class.

Use newspaper and tape to wrap small objects (buttons, acorns, stray keys, or pieces of candy) to serve as gifts. It's important the packages be small, about the same size, and unique. In one of the packages, place a folded one-dollar bill.

Also, arrange for two or three couples who have been married twenty years or longer to come to your meeting to be interviewed during the "www.asktheexperts.com" activity.

LEADER TIP for The Study

Because this topic can be so powerful and relevant to kids' lives, your group members may be tempted to get caught up in issues and lose sight of the deeper biblical principle found in The Point. Help your kids grasp The Point by guiding kids to focus on the biblical investigation and discussing how God's truth connects with reality in their lives.

Friendship First

LEADER TIP for The Study

Whenever groups discuss a list of questions, write the questions on newsprint, and tape the newsprint to the wall so groups can discuss the questions at their own pace.

THE STUDY

EXPERIENTIAL INTRODUCTION ▼

Gift-Wrapped Gizmos (5 to 10 minutes) Before the meeting, set out the wrapped packages you created earlier. As students arrive, ask them to select a package based *solely* on appearances—no shaking, sniffing, or squishing packages.

Ask students to hold their packages until everyone has one. Then, all together, ask students to unwrap their packages and take turns showing off their new acquisitions.

After the gifts are opened, say: **Do any of you wish you could trade your gift for something another person chose? If so, get ready! We'll take sixty seconds to let all those who want to trade try to work out a deal to get what they want. But no one *has* to trade. If you'd rather keep what you've got, don't trade it.**

When sixty seconds have passed, ask students to form trios and discuss these questions:

● **Why did you choose the package you did when you came into the room?**
● **Once you unwrapped your package, were you happy or disappointed? Explain.**
● **Did you trade? Why or why not?**
● **What do you wish you could have traded for?**

Form new trios and say, **Now I have three more questions for you to consider in your groups.**

● **How was selecting a package like dating?**
● **How was opening the package and seeing what was inside like dating?**
● **How was attempting to trade for something better like dating?**

Say: **When we decide to date someone, we're usually attracted to "outside" qualities, such as how the person looks, his or her sense of humor or athletic ability, or something else we can see from a distance.**

We begin dating without knowing what's inside the package—what the person believes, wants out of life, or thinks is important. Dating turns into a long process of hit and miss—and attempting to trade up for something better!

The Bible doesn't talk about dating. But it has a *lot* to say about relationships—and that includes relationships of the romantic kind. <u>Guys and girls can be good friends</u>, and today we'll discover how the Bible shows that building friendships is essential to finding true love.

Friendship First

BIBLE EXPLORATION ▼

The Ideal Date (20 to 25 minutes)

Form same-sex pairs or small groups. Give each group a plastic grocery bag, a permanent marker, and a stack of family magazines and newspapers.

Say: **You have two assignments. First, draw the face of your perfect date on the outside of the bag. Then using words and pictures from the printed materials, gather a bunch of items that describe the characteristics of a perfect date. Stuff them into the bag.**

For example, if you think honesty is an important characteristic, find a picture that symbolizes honesty and put it in the bag. However, no characteristic goes into your perfect-date bag unless your entire group agrees it's essential.

Give groups ten minutes to work. As kids begin, have them read John 13:34-35; Romans 12:10; and Romans 14:19 to glean ideas for qualities they'd like to see in a "perfect" date. When groups finish, ask them to take turns describing the characteristics of their perfect date.

Then ask:

● **Combine all these qualities, and you've got a perfect date, right? But how many of those qualities could you see by just *looking* at your perfect date?**

● **If you can't recognize these great qualities just by looking, how can you tell who has these wonderful qualities?**

Ask for suggestions, then say: **The only way to find out if a person has some qualities is to have a *relationship* with the person. You discover whether someone is kind by seeing how the person treats others. You find out whether someone is honest by watching how the person lives.**

The Bible says a lot about how to have relationships. Let's examine God's standards for relationships to discover how, even in the dating world, <u>guys and girls can be good friends</u>.

Have kids form new pairs or small groups that have a roughly equal number of guys and girls. Distribute Bibles and pens, and give each pair or small group a different section of the "Focus on Friendship" handout (pp. 53-54). (It's OK if some groups get the same section of the handout or if some groups get more than one section of the handout.) Ask the groups to look up the verses and read them together, then answer the questions listed after each verse.

When kids have finished, form a large circle, and have groups share with the whole class what they discovered. Then ask:

● **Based on what we've just learned, do you think it's best to date only people you know well? Why or why not?**

● **What would be the advantages of dating only friends?**

● **What would be the disadvantages of dating only the people you know well?**

● **What do you think is the purpose of dating?**

● **Do you think dating is an essential part of any romantic guy-girl relationship? Why or why not?**

● **Do you think <u>guys and girls can be good friends</u> and**

LEADER TIP for www.asktheexperts.com

In addition to interviewing married couples, consider asking several people who are divorced to also join the meeting. Then ask them the following questions:

● **What first attracted you to your mate?**

● **How important is it to be friends with your mate?**

● **How well did you know each other when you married?**

● **What advice would you give teenagers who are dating?**

choose not to date each other? Why or why not?
- How can the verses we've studied help you build strong relationships with the opposite sex?

👉 Say: **I think that <u>guys and girls can be good friends</u>. In fact, I think a good friendship is the best foundation for any good marriage. Let's test my theory to see if it's true.**

www.asktheexperts.com (10 to 15 minutes)

Invite in the couples you asked to join you for this part of the study. Once the couples are seated, have them introduce themselves and say how many years they've been married. Then interview the couples by asking:
- **What first attracted you to your mate?**
- **How important is it to be friends with your mate?**
- **How well did you know each other when you married?**
- **What's something you do now that helps you stay friends?**
- **What advice would you give teenagers who are dating?**

After you've asked these questions, allow time for kids to ask any follow-up questions they like. Then have kids applaud the couples for their successful marriages and thank them for coming. Once the couples are gone, have the kids discuss these questions:
- **What did you learn about friendship from these couples?**
- **How will you change the way you approach dating, based on what they said?**

👉 - **Based on all we've learned so far, we can see that <u>guys and girls can be good friends</u>. Why do you think it's important that the people you date should be your friends first?**

👉 Say: **Romance can happen between strangers. But true love is built on friendship. <u>Guys and girls can be good friends</u>—in fact, they must be in order for true love to grow.**

LEADER TIP for www.asktheexperts.com

Instead of interviewing the married couples at your meeting, try this creative option. Prior to your study, select several teenagers, and give them the following assignment: Using a video camera, interview couples in the church who have been married twenty years or longer. During the interview, ask each couple one or two of these questions:
- What first attracted you to your mate?
- How important is it to be friends with your mate?
- How well did you know each other when you married?
- What's something you do now that helps you stay friends?
- What advice would you give teenagers who are dating?

During the study, show clips from the interviews, then have kids discuss how the couples' comments show how <u>guys and girls can be good friends</u>.

DEPTH FINDER — UNDERSTANDING THE BIBLE

The verses kids examine in this study are a small sampling of the many Bible passages that teach Christians how to build strong relationships with one another. If you have time or want to continue this study in future sessions, consider exploring these other "relationship" verses with your kids:

Romans 12:13-15; 14:13; 15:1-7
Galatians 5:13-15
Ephesians 4:2-3, 25, 29-32
Colossians 3:12-16
1 Thessalonians 5:12-15
Hebrews 3:12-13; 10:24
James 4:11-12
1 Peter 1:22; 3:8
1 John 2:9-11

OBJECT LESSON CLOSING ▼

Mirror, Mirror, in My Hand (10 to 15 minutes) Gather kids in a circle. Say: **All people who come into our lives leave imprints. They may be good, bad, helpful, hurtful—but they leave impressions on us, just the same. It's as if each of us leaves fingerprints on others' lives.**

Pass a clean mirror around the circle. Instruct teenagers to each place a thumb print somewhere on the mirror.

As the mirror is passed around the circle, instruct each teenager to share a sentence prayer, asking God to help him or her be a positive influence on others—especially in dating relationships.

When the mirror has traveled around the circle once, send it back around once more so everyone can silently see his or her image in the "fingerprint" reflection. As they look at their images, have each student tell one way the person on his or her right has left a positive "imprint" on the student's life.

LEADER TIP

For Mirror, Mirror, in My Hand

Ask kids to wipe their thumbs on their foreheads before you send around the mirror so their thumb prints will show up clearly on the glass.

"A NEW COMMAND I GIVE YOU:

Love one another.

As I have loved you, so you must love one another.

All men will know that you are my disciples if you love one another."

—JOHN 13:34-35

Friendship First

Say: **When we're dating or just being friends, we leave an imprint. Let's live out our friendships and relationships so our imprints won't be painful when people see how we've impacted their lives.**

When the mirror reaches you again, say: **Let's close with one-word prayers. Please share a word that sums up what healthy relationships between Christians need to be. For example, you can say a word from the Bible passages you read or another word that would be appropriate. I'll open and close.**

Begin the prayer by saying: **God, please help me to be...**, then share one word such as "caring" or something similar. Then allow kids to share their one-word prayers.

DEPTHFINDER — UNDERSTANDING THESE KIDS

Think teaching about dating isn't necessary? Consider the following information: More than four out of five kids (82 percent) have had sexual relations with a member of the opposite sex by the age of nineteen. Before they even graduate from high school, one-fifth of all students will have had at least four sex partners. And if current trends continue, a majority of today's high school students will live with a partner prior to getting married.

(Source: George Barna, *Generation Next*)

Focus on Friendship

Cut apart these sections, and give one or more sections to each pair or small group.

JOHN 13:34-35

If you want your dating relationships to glorify God, what would you do on a typical date? What *wouldn't* you do?

What does it mean to love your date the way Jesus loves him or her?

---

1 TIMOTHY 5:2
(for guys)

How can you treat a young woman as a sister and still date her?

What does "absolute purity" mean?

---

1 PETER 3:3-4
(for girls)

Is this advice widely followed by most girls you know? Why or why not?

How will living by these values affect your dating life?

PHILIPPIANS 1:9-10

If you love someone you're dating, how might you build "knowledge and depth of insight" in your relationship?

Why did Paul think purity is important?

Permission to photocopy this handout from Group's Core Belief Bible Study Series granted for local church use.
Copyright © Group Publishing, Inc., P.O. Box 481, Loveland, CO 80539.

ROMANS 12:10

In what ways is it healthy to put others' needs before your own?

If you have "brotherly love" for someone you're dating, how might that affect the way you treat that person?

ROMANS 12:16

What are people proud of when they date? Why?

What does it mean to be conceited?

ROMANS 14:19

What sort of things could couples do on dates that meet this goal?

1 SAMUEL 16:7

How highly does God value looks? How does that compare with how you feel about how a potential date looks?

How would your description of your "perfect" date change if you didn't focus on appearances?

JAMES 5:16

Do you think people who are dating should confess their faults to each other? Why or why not?

why Active and Interactive Learning works with teenagers

Let's Start With the Big Picture

Think back to a major life lesson you've learned.
Got it? Now answer these questions:
- Did you learn your lesson from something you read?
- Did you learn it from something you heard?
- Did you learn it from something you experienced?

If you're like 99 percent of your peers, you answered "yes" only to the third question—you learned your life lesson from something you experienced.

This simple test illustrates the most convincing reason for using active and interactive learning with young people: People learn best through experience. Or to put it even more simply, people learn by doing.

Learning by doing is what active learning is all about. No more sitting quietly in chairs and listening to a speaker expound theories about God—that's passive learning. Active learning gets kids out of their chairs and into the experience of life. With active learning, kids get to *do* what they're studying. They *feel* the effects of the principles you teach. They *learn* by experiencing truth firsthand.

Active learning works because it recognizes three basic learning needs and uses them in concert to enable young people to make discoveries on their own and to find practical life applications for the truths they believe.

So what are these three basic learning needs?
1. Teenagers need action.
2. Teenagers need to think.
3. Teenagers need to talk.

Read on to find out exactly how these needs will be met by using the active and interactive learning techniques in Group's Core Belief Bible Study Series in your youth group.

1. Teenagers Need Action

Aircraft pilots know well the difference between passive and active learning. Their passive learning comes through listening to flight instructors and reading flight-instruction books. Their active learning comes through actually flying an airplane or flight simulator. Books and lectures may be helpful, but pilots really learn to fly by manipulating a plane's controls themselves.

We can help young people learn in a similar way. Though we may engage students passively in some reading and listening to teachers, their understanding and application of God's Word will really take off through simulated and real-life experiences.

Forms of active learning include simulation games; role-plays; service projects; experiments; research projects; group pantomimes; mock trials; construction projects; purposeful games; field trips; and, of course, the most powerful form of active learning—real-life experiences.

We can more fully explain active learning by exploring four of its characteristics:

- **Active learning is an adventure.** Passive learning is almost always predictable. Students sit passively while the teacher or speaker follows a planned outline or script.

In active learning, kids may learn lessons the teacher never envisioned. Because the leader trusts students to help create the learning experience, learners may venture into unforeseen discoveries. And often the teacher learns as much as the students.

- **Active learning is fun and captivating.** What are we communicating when we say, "OK, the fun's over—time to talk about God"? What's the hidden message? That joy is separate from God? And that learning is separate from joy?

What a shame.

Active learning is not joyless. One seventh-grader we interviewed clearly remembered her best Sunday school lesson: "Jesus was the light, and we went into a dark room and shut off the lights. We had a candle, and we learned that Jesus is the light and the dark can't shut off the light." That's active learning. Deena enjoyed the lesson. She had fun. And she learned.

Active learning intrigues people. Whether they find a foot-washing experience captivating or maybe a bit uncomfortable, they learn. And they learn on a level deeper than any work sheet or teacher's lecture could ever reach.

- **Active learning involves everyone.** Here the difference between passive and active learning becomes abundantly clear. It's like the difference between watching a football game on television and actually playing in the game.

The "trust walk" provides a good example of involving everyone in active learning. Half of the group members put on blindfolds; the other half serve as guides. The "blind" people trust the guides to lead them through the building or outdoors. The guides prevent the blind people from falling down stairs or tripping over rocks. Everyone needs to participate to learn the inherent lessons of trust, faith, doubt, fear, confidence, and servanthood. Passive spectators of this experience would learn little, but participants learn a great deal.

- **Active learning is focused through debriefing.** Activity simply for activity's sake doesn't usually result in good learning. Debriefing—evaluating an experience by discussing it in pairs or small groups—helps focus the experience and draw out its meaning. Debriefing helps sort and order the information students gather during the experience. It helps learners relate the recently experienced activity to their lives.

The process of debriefing is best started immediately after an experience. We use a three-step process in debriefing: reflection, interpretation, and application.

Reflection—This first step asks the students, "How did you feel?" Active-learning experiences typically evoke an emotional reaction, so it's appropriate to begin debriefing at that level.

Some people ask, "What do feelings have to do with education?" Feelings have everything to do with education. Think back again to that time in your life when you learned a big lesson. In all likelihood, strong feelings accompanied that lesson. Our emotions tend to cement things into our memories.

When you're debriefing, use open-ended questions to probe feelings. Avoid questions that can be answered with a "yes" or "no." Let your learners know that there are no wrong answers to these "feeling" questions. Everyone's feelings are valid.

Interpretation—The next step in the debriefing process asks, "What does this mean to you? How is this experience like or unlike some other aspect of your life?" Now you're asking people to identify a message or principle from the experience.

You want your learners to discover the message for themselves. So instead of telling students your answers, take the time to ask questions that encourage self-discovery. Use Scripture and discussion in pairs or small groups to explore how the actions and effects of the activity might translate to their lives.

Alert! Some of your people may interpret wonderful messages that you never intended. That's not failure! That's the Holy Spirit at work. God allows us to catch different glimpses of his kingdom even when we all look through the same glass.

Application—The final debriefing step asks, "What will you do about it?" This step moves learning into action. Your young people have shared a common experience. They've discovered a principle. Now they must create something new with what they've just experienced and interpreted. They must integrate the message into their lives.

The application stage of debriefing calls for a decision. Ask your students how they'll change, how they'll grow, what they'll do as a result of your time together.

2. Teenagers Need to Think

Today's students have been trained not to think. They aren't dumber than previous generations. We've simply conditioned them not to use their heads.

You see, we've trained our kids to respond with the simplistic answers they think the teacher wants to hear. Fill-in-the-blank student workbooks and teachers who ask dead-end questions such as "What's the capital of Delaware?" have produced kids and adults who have learned not to think.

And it doesn't just happen in junior high or high school. Our children are schooled very early not to think. Teachers attempt to help kids read with nonsensical fill-in-the-blank drills, word scrambles, and missing-letter puzzles.

Helping teenagers think requires a paradigm shift in how we teach. We need to plan for and set aside time for higher-order thinking and be willing to reduce our time spent on lower-order parroting. Group's Core Belief Bible Study Series is designed to help you do just that.

Thinking classrooms look quite different from traditional classrooms. In most church environments, the teacher does most of the talking and hopes that knowledge will transmit from his or her brain to the students'. In thinking settings, the teacher coaches students to ponder, wonder, imagine, and problem-solve.

3. Teenagers Need to Talk

Everyone knows that the person who learns the most in any class is the teacher. Explaining a concept to someone else is usually more helpful to the explainer than to the listener. So why not let the students do more teaching? That's one of the chief benefits of letting kids do the talking. This process is called interactive learning.

What is interactive learning? Interactive learning occurs when students discuss and work cooperatively in pairs or small groups.

Interactive learning encourages learners to work together. It honors the fact that students can learn from one another, not just from the teacher. Students work together in pairs or small groups to accomplish shared goals. They build together, discuss together, and present together. They teach each other and learn from one another. Success as a group is celebrated. Positive interdependence promotes individual and group learning.

Interactive learning not only helps people learn but also helps learners feel better about themselves and get along better with others. It accomplishes these things more effectively than the independent or competitive methods.

Here's a selection of interactive learning techniques that are used in Group's Core Belief Bible Study Series. With any of these models, leaders may assign students to specific partners or small groups. This will maximize cooperation and learning by preventing all the "rowdies" from linking up. And it will allow for new friendships to form outside of established cliques.

Following any period of partner or small-group work, the leader may reconvene the entire class for large-group processing. During this time the teacher may ask for reports or discoveries from individuals or teams. This technique builds in accountability for the teacherless pairs and small groups.

Pair-Share—With this technique each student turns to a partner and responds to a question or problem from the teacher or leader. Every learner responds. There are no passive observers. The teacher may then ask people to share their partners' responses.

Study Partners—Most curricula and most teachers call for Scripture passages to be read to the whole class by one person. One reads; the others doze.

Why not relinquish some teacher control and let partners read and react with each other? They'll all be involved—and will learn more.

Learning Groups—Students work together in small groups to create a model, design artwork, or study a passage or story; then they discuss what they learned through the experience. Each person in the learning group may be assigned a specific role. Here are some examples:

Reader

Recorder (makes notes of key thoughts expressed during the reading or discussion)

Checker (makes sure everyone understands and agrees with answers arrived at by the group)

Encourager (urges silent members to share their thoughts)

When everyone has a specific responsibility, knows what it is, and contributes to a small group, much is accomplished and much is learned.

Summary Partners—One student reads a paragraph, then the partner summarizes the paragraph or interprets its meaning. Partners alternate roles with each paragraph.

The paraphrasing technique also works well in discussions. Anyone who wishes to share a thought must first paraphrase what the previous person said. This sharpens listening skills and demonstrates the power of feedback communication.

Jigsaw—Each person in a small group examines a different concept, Scripture, or part of an issue. Then each teaches the others in the group. Thus, all members teach, and all must learn the others' discoveries. This technique is called a jigsaw because individuals are responsible to their group for different pieces of the puzzle.

JIGSAW EXAMPLE

Here's an example of a jigsaw.

Assign four-person teams. Have teammates each number off from one to four. Have all the Ones go to one corner of the room, all the Twos to another corner, and so on.

Tell team members they're responsible for learning information in their numbered corners and then for teaching their team members when they return to their original teams.

Give the following assignments to various groups:

Ones: Read Psalm 22. Discuss and list the prophecies made about Jesus.

Twos: Read Isaiah 52:13–53:12. Discuss and list the prophecies made about Jesus.

Threes: Read Matthew 27:1-32. Discuss and list the things that happened to Jesus.

Fours: Read Matthew 27:33-66. Discuss and list the things that happened to Jesus.

After the corner groups meet and discuss, instruct all learners to return to their original teams and report what they've learned. Then have each team determine which prophecies about Jesus were fulfilled in the passages from Matthew.

Call on various individuals in each team to report one or two prophecies that were fulfilled.

You Can Do It Too!

All this information may sound revolutionary to you, but it's really not. God has been using active and interactive learning to teach his people for generations. Just look at Abraham and Isaac, Jacob and Esau, Moses and the Israelites, Ruth and Boaz. And then there's Jesus, who used active learning all the time!

Group's Core Belief Bible Study Series makes it easy for you to use active and interactive learning with your group. The active and interactive elements are automatically built in! Just follow the outlines, and watch as your kids grow through experience and positive interaction with others.

> **FOR DEEPER STUDY**
>
> For more information on incorporating active and interactive learning into your work with teenagers, check out these resources:
>
> ● *Why Nobody Learns Much of Anything at Church: And How to Fix It,* by Thom and Joani Schultz (Group Publishing) and
> ● *Do It! Active Learning in Youth Ministry,* by Thom and Joani Schultz (Group Publishing).

your evaluation of

Bible Study Series
for junior high/middle school

the truth about
RELATIONSHIPS

Group Publishing, Inc.
Attention: Core Belief Talk-Back
P.O. Box 481
Loveland, CO 80539
Fax: (970) 679-4370

Please help us continue to provide innovative and useful resources for ministry. After you've led the studies in this volume, take a moment to fill out this evaluation; then mail or fax it to us at the address above. Thanks!

● ● ● ● ● ●

1. As a whole, this book has been (circle one)

not very helpful   very helpful
1   2   3   4   5   6   7   8   9   10

2. The best things about this book:

3. How this book could be improved:

4. What I will change because of this book:

5. Would you be interested in field-testing future Core Belief Bible Studies and giving us your feedback? If so, please complete the information below:

Name _____

Street address _____

City _____ State _____ Zip _____

Daytime telephone (____) _____ Date _____

THANKS!

Permission to photocopy this evaluation from Group's Core Belief Bible Study Series granted for local church use.
Copyright © Group Publishing, Inc., P.O. Box 481, Loveland, CO 80539.

Bible Study Series

Give Your Teenagers a Solid Faith Foundation That Lasts a Lifetime!

Here are the *essentials* of the Christian life—core values teenagers *must* believe to make good decisions now...and build an *unshakable* lifelong faith. Developed by youth workers like you...field-tested with *real* youth groups in *real* churches...here's the meat your kids *must* have to grow spiritually—presented in a fun, involving way!

Each 4-session **Core Belief Bible Study Series** book lets you easily...
- Lead deep, compelling, *relevant* discussions your kids won't want to miss...
- Involve teenagers in exploring life-changing truths...
- Help kids create healthy relationships with each other—and you!

Plus you'll make an *eternal difference* in the lives of your kids as you give them a solid faith foundation that stands firm on God's Word.

Here are the Core Belief Bible Study Series titles already available...

Senior High Studies

Title	ISBN
Why **Authority** Matters	0-7644-0892-5
Why **Being a Christian** Matters	0-7644-0883-6
Why **Creation** Matters	0-7644-0880-1
Why **Forgiveness** Matters	0-7644-0887-9
Why **God** Matters	0-7644-0874-7
Why **God's Justice** Matters	0-7644-0886-0
Why **Jesus Christ** Matters	0-7644-0875-5
Why **Love** Matters	0-7644-0889-5
Why **Our Families** Matter	0-7644-0894-1
Why **Personal Character** Matters	0-7644-0885-2
Why **Prayer** Matters	0-7644-0893-3
Why **Relationships** Matter	0-7644-0896-8
Why **Serving Others** Matters	0-7644-0895-X
Why **Spiritual Growth** Matters	0-7644-0884-4
Why **Suffering** Matters	0-7644-0879-8
Why **the Bible** Matters	0-7644-0882-8
Why **the Church** Matters	0-7644-0890-9
Why **the Holy Spirit** Matters	0-7644-0876-3
Why **the Last Days** Matter	0-7644-0888-7
Why **the Spiritual Realm** Matters	0-7644-0881-X
Why **Worship** Matters	0-7644-0891-7

Junior High/Middle School Studies

Title	ISBN
The Truth About **Authority**	0-7644-0868-2
The Truth About **Being a Christian**	0-7644-0859-3
The Truth About **Creation**	0-7644-0856-9
The Truth About **Developing Character**	0-7644-0861-5
The Truth About **God**	0-7644-0850-X
The Truth About **God's Justice**	0-7644-0862-3
The Truth About **Jesus Christ**	0-7644-0851-8
The Truth About **Love**	0-7644-0865-8
The Truth About **Our Families**	0-7644-0870-4
The Truth About **Prayer**	0-7644-0869-0
The Truth About **Relationships**	0-7644-0872-0
The Truth About **Serving Others**	0-7644-0871-2
The Truth About **Sin and Forgiveness**	0-7644-0863-1
The Truth About **Spiritual Growth**	0-7644-0860-7
The Truth About **Suffering**	0-7644-0855-0
The Truth About **the Bible**	0-7644-0858-5
The Truth About **the Church**	0-7644-0899-2
The Truth About **the Holy Spirit**	0-7644-0852-6
The Truth About **the Last Days**	0-7644-0864-X
The Truth About **the Spiritual Realm**	0-7644-0857-7
The Truth About **Worship**	0-7644-0867-4

Order today from your local Christian bookstore, or write:
Group Publishing, P.O. Box 485, Loveland, CO 80539.

Exciting Resources for Your Youth Ministry

All-Star Games From All-Star Youth Leaders

The ultimate game book—from the biggest names in youth ministry! All-time no-fail favorites from Wayne Rice, Les Christie, Rich Mullins, Tiger McLuen, Darrell Pearson, Dave Stone, Bart Campolo, Steve Fitzhugh, and 21 others! You get all the games you'll need for any situation. Plus, you get practical advice about how to design your own games and tricks for turning a *good* game into a *great* game!

ISBN 0-7644-2020-8

Last Impressions: Unforgettable Closings for Youth Meetings

Make the closing moments of your youth programs powerful and memorable with this collection of Group's best-ever low-prep (or no-prep!) youth meeting closings. You get over 170 favorite closings, each tied to a thought-provoking Bible passage. Great for anyone who works with teenagers!

ISBN 1-55945-629-9

The Youth Worker's Encyclopedia of Bible-Teaching Ideas

Here are the most comprehensive idea-books available for youth workers. With more than 365 creative ideas in each of these 400-page encyclopedias, there's at least one idea for every book of the Bible. You'll find ideas for retreats and overnighters...learning games...adventures...special projects...affirmations...parties...prayers...music...devotions...skits...and more!

Old Testament ISBN 1-55945-184-X
New Testament ISBN 1-55945-183-1

PointMaker™ Devotions for Youth Ministry

These 45 PointMakers™ help your teenagers discover, understand, and apply biblical principles. Use PointMakers as brief meetings on specific topics or slide them into any youth curriculum to make a lasting impression. Includes handy Scripture and topical indexes that make it quick and easy to select the perfect PointMaker for any lesson you want to teach!

ISBN 0-7644-2003-8

Order today from your local Christian bookstore, or write: Group Publishing, P.O. Box 485, Loveland, CO 80539